You Who?
Group Discussion
Study Guide

Published by Canon Press
P.O. Box 8729, Moscow, Idaho 83843
800.488.2034 | www.canonpress.com

Canon Press, *You Who? Group Discussion Study Guide*
Copyright ©2019 by Canon Press.

Cover design by James Engerbretson
Interior design by Valerie Anne Bost

Printed in the United States of America.

Library of Congress Cataloging-in-Publication Data

You who? : group discussion study guide / Rachel Jankovic
Moscow : Canon Press, 2019.
LCCN 2019011318 | ISBN 9781947644960 (pbk. : alk. paper)
LCSH: Jankovic, Rachel. You who? | Identity (Psychology)--Religious aspects--Christianity--Study and teaching.
LCC BV4509.5 .J363 2019 | DDC 233--dc23
LC record available at https://lccn.loc.gov/2019011318

1

TROUBLE, TRUTH, AND GLORY

Summary:
Rather than listening to the lies of the world about our identity, we should remember that our identity is completely rooted in Christ.

Highlights:
"If you are looking for a book that will gently pet your bangs and soothe your worried brow, telling you how beautiful you are, this is not it.... This book is not here to help you in your quest

for self-love. I want something much, much better for you, because I want something true for you." (1-2)

"If you won't face the fact that we have sin, there will be no joy in looking to a Savior." (2)

"That is the basis of all my belonging. He knows who I am. He knows where I belong. Nothing more than that.... Nothing but God: He mine, and I His." (7)

Questions for Discussion and Application:
1. What does Rachel say her goal in this book is? Does she say hard words just because she gets a kick out of it?

2. What does Rachel give as the reasons why she has never doubted her identity? What are some of the things that God has given to you that have helped you stay on the straight path?

3. Why don't we need to plot and scheme to achieve "self-actualization"? Do you know any-one who is clearly anxious or perpetually dis-content because of this quest to find him or herself?

4. How can this book benefit you, whether you are already secure in your Christian identity or not?

Study the Word:

Read 2 Corinthians 2. Why did Paul say hard things to the Corinthians? What was his goal? Imitating him, how must we treat brothers who have sinned or are confused?

2

FOOLISHNESS

Summary:
We Christians have often carelessly adopted the unbelieving philosophy of our culture.

Highlights:
"Regular, honest people buy unbelievably foolish philosophy, but they buy it toned down and in the clearance bins. That is why we don't recognize it right away for the monstrosity it is." (12)

"If we could just see the belief systems we are buying into spelled out in plain writing in the catalog or on the philosophical runway (so to speak), it might shock us. This is not the clothing of our people, and these are not the words we should want on our foreheads." (13-14)

Questions for Discussion and Application:
1. Does Rachel think that all philosophy is bad? What is the great danger here?

2. How do Christians get tricked into fads and ideas that we would usually see through? Consider the latest clothing fashions or the most recent movies you have seen other people seemingly like, despite bad ideas.

3. Most people assume that there is no God and that we are the result of millions of years of accidents. How does this shape culture today?

4. Have you noticed other unbelieving assumptions that shape how we live our lives?

Study the Word:
Read Colossians 2. In v. 8, what are we supposed to beware of? How is Jesus the solution to vain philosophy?

3

A PHILOSOPHY STARTER

Summary:
Modern philosophy doesn't have a coherent definition of the self, wanting to locate it in our physical selves, such as in brains or memories. The Bible says that humans are defined by the fact that God has given each one of us a body and an eternal soul together, which bears His image.

Highlights:

"We believe that we were made with a soul. We believe that our physical bodies are not the whole story. We have an identity that is spoken by God, sustained by God, and even our physical body replaces itself according to God's design. At the end of the day we aren't merely mortal, but eternal beings." (22)

"When you remove the role of the active Creator from the discussion, you are left with a bunch of human component parts that have no direction and make no sense." (23)

Questions for Discussion and Application:

1. Why is it important to know about all these philosophers?

2. What is the problem of Theseus's ship? What are the essential things about you that form your identity? (Hint: they're not located in what you like or what you've done.)

3. What is wrong with the belief that it is our memory or brains that make us human? How does this issue affect groups of people like

infants, children, the elderly, or those with disabilities?

4. How does God view your body and your soul?

Study the Word:
Read Acts 17:22-34. How does Paul respond to the philosophers of his day? Did he know about their philosophy? How should we study philosophy in light of Paul's apologetic here?

4

SORTING OUT SARTRE

Summary:
Sartre was a philosopher who said that existence precedes essence, meaning basically that we need to create our self. His completely immoral and self-serving life shows us what this philosophy looks like, lived out consistently.

Highlights:
"In the assumed absence of God the Father, Sartre stepped up to tell us all how to be—what we are for, how to go about becoming more,

etc. He stood in for God the Father for us and explained us to us. And we listened." (33)

"If you are setting out to remodel a home that has rotten floorboards, one of the first steps must be an evaluation of the extent of the damage." (40)

Questions for Discussion and Application:
1. What does it mean to say that "existence precedes essence"?

2. How is the idea that "you can make yourself" philosophically incoherent?

3. Why do you think Sartre saw belief in God as not just false, but irrelevant? How did Sartre change what we think is and is not important today? Do you know unbelievers who think of Christianity as not so much false as irrelevant?

4. Why was Sartre so attractive to the people of France at that time? Why do you think, in America's current social context, this lie is so easily believed?

5. Do you have other examples of movies, songs, celebrities, or other bits of pop culture that talk about "creating your own meaning" or "following your heart"?

Study the Word:

Read 2 Cor. 11. How does Paul argue against the false apostles (v. 12)? Does he just appeal to arguments or does he appeal to their lives and works as well? How about his own life and works?

5

THE PINNACLE
THAT ISN'T

Summary:
Maslow argued that people have a hierarchy of needs, and that they need to meet all their needs in order to achieve self-actualization, whereas Jesus tells us not to worry about our needs or to seek our self's good first and foremost, but instead to seek to serve and glorify God.

Highlight:

"Do we marry and have children to better meet our own needs? The answer is a resounding "No, we don't!" What could go wrong here, other than everything?" (46)

"In Christianity, the self is always a tool and never a destination." (48)

"[Maslow] didn't know God, and that means on a fundamental level he could not know man." (49)

Questions for Discussion and Application:

1. Have you seen Maslow's hierarchy of needs before? Before now, has it made sense to you intuitively?

2. Are all the things that Maslow sees as needs bad things to pursue? If not, what is the difference between how a Christian pursues them and how an unbeliever pursues them?

3. Do people actually pursue their needs in the straightforward step-by-step way as described by Maslow? Why do you think people are obsessed with these kinds of charts and schematics, despite their artificiality?

4. Have you been caught up in believing that you need to move on to the next stage of Maslow's hierarchy, lest you fail in your self-actualization?

Study the Word:

Read Matthew 6:19-34. What does Jesus say about seeking even the lowest level of Maslow's hierarchy of needs? Does Jesus say that we are supposed to be without needs at all (v. 32)? Is it possible to put Christian priorities into a "hierarchy"? (Hint: Consider Jesus's words on the greatest commandment.)

6

THE NARRATIVE OF YOU

Summary:
Today's adults are taught that they can go into the world and choose who they are. This may seem harmless but actually leads us to idolize freedom, choice, and our ability to define who we are above any other relationships or priorities.

Highlights:
"We think we are making ourselves from scratch, and we love to admire our work." (54)

"If you believe that some people actually have a head start, not just in status and careers and schooling, but in actual personhood, what a horrible unfairness it would be. And what would that mean for us?" (56)

"If your essence is in your choices, anything that takes away your own free will and choices is obviously the enemy." (57)

Questions for Discussion and Application:
1. How does the narrative of the self make us think about accomplishments and hobbies? How does a Christian view of these things differ?

2. Why is it that at this moment in history, so much of our lives is controllable and can be shaped by our own preferences?

3. Many people believe that poverty prevents people from achieving their potential. How does this idea shape the political and cultural discussion around poverty and class in America?

4. Explain from this chapter why so many people are willing to argue that killing an unborn

baby is a natural right. Could this argument be applied to the just-born infant?

5. Have you put freedom, choice, or the ability to define who you are above direct commands God has given you?

Study the Word:
Read Philippians 3. What has Paul given up for the sake of Christ? Were the things that he was giving up all bad? Where does Paul find his identity?

7

A CHAPTER OF HATE

Summary:
Because individuals believe that they each have the right to tell their own story, Christians who refuse to play along with these life-views, instead proclaiming God's view (that is, proclaiming reality), are "hateful." In the post-Sartre world, this is because God's view contradicts people's most fundamental right to be who and what they want to be.

Highlights:
"If the Christian idea about identity is right, then all the self-constructed people in the world have just been building their little selves out in the thin air off the cliff edge like so many Wile E. Coyotes. The bottom isn't about to fall out from under them because it has never been there at all. There is no safety, there is no refuge, there is no security. It is understandable that all they can see in our Christian claims is hate." (67)

"It doesn't matter how long or thoughtful or detailed the story you are writing is. If it is written by a character in the story rather than the Author of the story, it can only ever be tiny; it will always be minuscule by comparison. You cannot, as a character, outwrite the Author of you." (68)

Questions for Discussion and Application:
1. How do people use "counter-cultural" symbols to pretend that they are not blindly following the culture?

2. Describe how the "narrative of the self" incentivizes and even encourages gay marriage, transgender surgery, and all sorts of contemporary

weirdness. Why do you think these kinds of thing are more common nowadays compared to a hundred years ago?

3. Former Supreme Court Justice Anthony Kennedy wrote in the case that legalized gay marriage, "At the heart of liberty is the right to define one's own concept of existence, of meaning, of the universe, and of the mystery of human life." Given this kind of progressive thinking, why is "choice" such a big deal in our culture? What might be the problem with phrases like "family values" and "freedom"?

4. Do you have family or friends who are telling a story about themselves that is contrary to the story God is telling? What happens when you tell them the truth?

Study the Word:
Read John 15:18-25. Why do people see so much of what Christians say as hatred? Pop culture tends to consider Jesus to be a smiling flower-child. Why would anyone want to crucify that? What made the Jews want to kill him (Jn. 3:19; 7:7; Matt. 22:13-39)?

HALFSIES

Summary:
Christians try to add Jesus like a cherry on top of the self-created milkshake of their life. But God never settles for half: He wants your whole life, which means that much of what we consider our identity has to die.

Highlights:
"The self-created you and the God-created you do not go together like ham and eggs, peanut butter and jam, or wine and cheese. They go

together more like a living body with a dead limb." (70)

"But Christ will not be managed or contained like that. If He truly bought you with His blood, He did not do so in order to get a sponsorship position in your life. He is not here to look good next to your brand. He bought your life, and you are His." (70-71)

"If our own little interests are the same size in our life as our Savior and our God, there are only two possibilities. One is that your Savior is becoming rather tiny—as insignificant as any other news about you. The other option is that fashion or show poodles or oils is rising to idol-atrous levels in your life." (71)

Questions for Discussion and Application:
1. Why do you think Christians are tempted to make our faith a product that unbelievers can buy rather than a command that people can heed or ignore?

2. How much time do you give to prayer, Scripture, and praising God? How much does that compare with your biggest hobbies?

3. Many people bemoan today's consumerist society, but are helpless to change it. Why do people care so much about what they buy?

4. What is the problem with many Christian slogans today like "Let go, and let God"? How is that different from Jesus' command to leave everything and follow Him?

5. Have you tried to make Jesus part of your personal "brand"?

Study the Word:
Read Mark 10:17-31. Do you think that Jesus wanted all his followers to be poor? What kind of discipleship are we called to? How should we think of our identity in light of this?

9

THE WORSHIPER

Summary:

We need an identity that is rooted in something bigger than ourselves, and that identity needs to ultimately be as a worshiper of God who glorifies and serves Him.

Highlights:

"In order to satisfy myself, who I am must in some way be greater than myself." (81)

"You are to live to the glory of God. Every minute—all of them, for His glory. Is this a sufficient answer to our hearts' questions? I believe it is. This is an answer that may leave us with more questions, but it is more questions that will in turn have real answers." (82)

"God is our glory. God is the glory of sinners, the glory of failures." (84)

Questions for Discussion and Application:
1. Why are society's answers to the problem of identity so superficial? How do people in our culture display a longing for more "transcendent" answers?

2. What does it mean that man is made to be a worshiper?

3. How are we freed by the knowledge that our story isn't actually about us?

4. Tell your life story. How does that story glorify God? When you pray, do you thank God for the events that have happened in your life? How can your life be greater than the sum of its parts?

Study the Word:

Read John 6:25-71. What are the ways in which we feed on Christ (vv. 29, 63; cf. 4:34)? How do you live in such a way that you are constantly feeding on Christ?

10

PLANTING FLAGS

Summary:

Our lives do matter, and we do need to tell our story: however our story should be defined by being obedient, and we can remind ourselves of this by constantly planting flags; in other words, we should constantly be reminding ourselves about who we are and endeavoring to give the glory to God.

"We are the worshipers, and we are not the worshiped. We are characters, and He is the Author. God is great, and we are not." (87)

"We have our hands full of little troubles, but they are little troubles that matter to the Maker of the universe." (88)

"Your trouble at work, your need to clean the bathroom and make dinner, your difficult conversation with a friend—this is all part of the greatest story." (89)

Questions for Discussion and Application:
1. How does believing in God help us see both how small and large our lives are (cf. Ps. 8:4; 56:8)?

2. How do we normally think of the story of our lives? Do we think more about all the things we are experiencing or about whether we are living for God's glory?

3. What do we normally pray for? How does this compare to what Paul prays for (1 Cor. 1:4-9, Eph. 1:15-23; Phil. 1:9-11; Col. 1:10-14; 2 Thess. 1:11-12; Philemon 1:6)?

4. Why do even Christians feel bitter when their lives aren't going the way they hoped? How does David deal with situations like these in the Psalms?

5. What does it mean to "plant flags"? What are times when you are normally anxious or have a hard time remembering God? How can you remember in those moments of crisis to plant flags?

Study the Word:
Read Philippians 3:1, 4:4-9. Why is it important that we constantly remind ourselves of the goodness of God? What does the peace of God do for us? How does Paul value time and habits of the mind?

11

A NEW GLORY

Summary:
We often avoid simple obedience by thinking that we actually need to be focused on doing jaw-dropping things for God; instead, we need to focus on what is right in front of us, small or great.

Highlights:
"No obedience to the Lord will ever go out into the void to continue to be useless into eternity.

Things are happening; nothing is in vain. Your small obedience means something." (97-98)

"We tend think of the virtue of contentment as being a great dud..... But contentment and gratitude, some of the smallest seeds, grow some of the biggest trees." (99-100)

"The Christian's cup is not full of difficult situations or important opportunities or even feelings. The Christian's cup is full of Christ. Always full, always overflowing." (100)

Questions for Discussion and Application:
1. Are Christians really driven to do great things for God through being discontent with ordinary duties?

2. People often point to verses where Jesus tells us to take up our crosses and follow him, and use it to guilt Christians who are living normal lives. What is the problem with this?

3. What are some labors that you usually don't think God is going to reward you for doing? What is the Bible's view of that kind of obedience (Matt. 10:42)?

4. Why do people think that contentment is a boring virtue? Do you pray that God would give you contentment with your spouse (or lack thereof), with your duties, with your friends, with your situation, or with your me-time?

5. What are some specific times and circumstances when you are tempted to discontentment?

Study the Word:
Read Phil. 4:10-20. How has Paul learned contentment? Why does Paul ask the church of Philippians to give to him? Who will supply our need?

12

HANGING ON

Summary:

Christians often think that following God means looking to our feelings for clues as to whether we are walking with Him; this is nonsense, and again we should simply focus on being obedient, even if we don't feel fulfilled all the time.

Highlights:

"the way we can know that we are doing what we are supposed to be doing is actually very simple. Are you obeying God? Are you honoring

Him? Are you being content and rejoicing in your lot? Congratulations! You have tremendous purpose and clarity and calling. This is it." (109-110)

"Read the Word. Obey the Word. Obey it now. Obey it again." (113)

"This is a call to grab the handle of the great gardening machine called obedience and let the glory of God power you through a great number of three-inch tree trunks. Hang on, obey Him, watch the chips fly, feel them sting on your shins, and occasionally look behind you to see the beauty that God is accomplishing in your obedience, because it will be genuinely glorious." (113)

Questions for Discussion and Application:
1. God has not revealed the specific route by which we are going to serve Him in life. Why does this fact make Christians often try to "figure out God's will for their lives" or make them feel lost and aimless?

2. What is the danger of looking to our own inclinations for clues as to how to best glorify

God? Why do we often think that our feelings are an indicator of whether we are being fruitful or not? How does the way our society encourages us to build our careers and lifestyles encourage discontentment?

3. Again, how do we justify our lack of contentment? Why do people talk about "settling for less" as though it were a bad thing?

4. How can we focus on obedience, rather than allow ourselves to be constantly frustrated by using our feelings to figure out whether we are doing the right thing? How is the Christian life so much easier and so much harder than we think?

Study the Word:
Read Hebrews 11. How did all of these people not see the final result of their obedience? Did they receive the promise? How should we expect our life's work to look like at times?

GLORY GIVERS

Summary:
We are not made to pursue our own glory; instead, we should always seek to glorify God, getting glory from Him as a result.

Highlights:
"We have a natural, God-given desire for glory, but it must have a healthy purpose. Glory to give, not glory to hoard. Glory to pass on." (115-116)

"Learning to live your life as a sacrifice is learning to be as close to God as you possibly can be, all of the time. This is the point. Be near to Him when you eat your dinner for His glory. Be near to Him when you take your dog on a walk. Be near to Him when you do anything you do, all the days of your life." (117)

Questions for Discussion and Application:

1. What are the kinds of glory that people pursue today? How are these kinds of glory fleeting and ultimately not satisfying?

2. For the Christian, what is the path to glorification?

3. What does God promise to give us when we give Him glory? Do you think the promise of pleasure is just something we get in heaven, or is it found in this life?

4. What are some places in your life where you are faced with a hard decision? How can you evaluate which option brings more glory to God?

Study the Word:

Read John 7:18, 8:50; 2 Cor. 3:18, 10:7-18. What do these passages say about glory? How do we gain it? What is the problem with glorying in oneself? What does Paul use as an example of false glorying?

14

ASKING FOR LESS

Summary:

We often think that if we just had time to relax, someone who constantly told us they cared
about us, or some regular source of recognition,
then we'd have what we need—all this despite
the fact that God cares about us, died for us,
and is the bread of life for us. Jesus is enough.

Highlights:

"Christ is more than you ever wanted. He answers the need you are feeling around in the

dark to fill, and He answers it in a way that will deal with it forever. In fact, He answers whatever need you have in such a way that you are transformed forever." (128-9)

"We wanted a thoughtfully timed coffee, not cleansing blood and the everlasting arms. We wanted someone to say, "I care about you" on a postit note, not someone to give their life for us." (130)

"We need to open our hands that are full of little requests, little needs, and drop them all so that we might, with both hands and whole hearts embrace He who is so much more." (132)

Questions for Discussion and Application:
1. Why do you think so many people feel isolation, loneliness, and depression these days? How did Jesus deal with agony of spirit (Lk. 22:42-44)?

2. From this chapter, what are the two things we need to do to find ourselves? Do you think of obedience like a nasty vegetable? What are ways you can change how you think about this virtue?

3. In what situations have you been tempted to feel that God was "not enough"? Why do you think it's so easy to think that if we only had more of _____ [fill in the blank], life would be so much better? What are the ways our culture reinforces this narrative?

Study the Word:
Read 1 Cor. 1:18-31 and 2 Cor. 11:16-33. How did God surprise the world in how He redeemed it? What about it was especially problematic for the Greeks and Jews? What are ways in which Paul's life appeared foolish to the world? How would people today say it is foolish to think that Christ is enough?

LOST BOYS

Summary:
We are constantly told that if we believe in ourselves, we will do whatever we set out to do;
instead, we need to believe in God and live in
humble obedience to Him.

Highlights:
"The world has switched out the depth and
richness and glory of believing entirely in another for your salvation, and they have replaced
it with lame attempts at self-worship and

self-identity. This is the philosophical version of carob chips, only a thousand times less satisfying." (138-9)

"The world offers therapy, advice books, and support groups, and promotes many false ways to self-actualization. Despite so many people buying into this, it is a miserable job. When they manage to kneel, they find the altar is empty, and when they manage to clamber up on the altar there are no worshipers." (141)

Questions for Discussion and Application:
1. What happens to worshipers of idols (Ps. 115)? How do you think this plays out with the idols of today?

2. What is so compelling about the idea of just believing in yourself? Do you think it's ever helped people get stuff done?

3. Have you ever known someone who was constantly trying to improve themselves? Does this explain why a lot of people are desperate and unhappy? Do you know any believers who are unhappy in this way? At the same time, can

you learn anything useful from these obsessive people?

Study the Word:
Read Psalm 115. Why did people trust in idols? Why does the Psalmist mock them? What are the ways in which people are damaged by idolatry?

16

UNCONCERNED

Summary:
Even though we change, God does not. Thus, we should not focus on who we are or what we are becoming, but instead make our focus God-ward, which counterintuitively will give our view of self a stable, unchanging foundation.

Highlights:
"For the Christian, the question of 'Who am I?' is actually just another way of asking 'Who is He?'" (143)

"Because we are becoming ourselves through responsive obedience to God we do not need either ourselves or our situations to be settled." (147)

"Our very selves [are] the tools with which we strive to serve God." (149)

Questions for Discussion and Application:
1. What does James say we should do as a result of God's unchanging nature (Jas. 1:17-21)? How does the author of Hebrews say we should live, since Jesus is the same yesterday, today, and tomorrow (Heb. 13:8-9)?

2. How does the Bible encourage us to see old age (Prov. 16:31)? What kinds of things should we look forward to as we age?

3. How should we deal with seasons of life in which we have less time to relax? When and why does something like the modern "self-care" fad go too far?

4. How does the New Testament talk about sanctification (Gal. 4:19; Eph. 3:17; Col. 1:27)? Are we to be self-forgetful?

Study the Word:
2 Corinthians 1:8-11, 12:7-10. How did the events of Paul's life change how he saw his situation? How did the bad occurrences bring him to obedience?

BE MADE NEW

Summary:

Our personality traits are not things that define us or excuse our weaknesses; instead they are the material we work with so that we can grow.

Highlights:

"The knowledge of who you are is connected not to revelation of that fact at some point (like the results of a personality test), but rather to obedience" (156)

"Far from our personalities being like eye color (something you are born with and can't do anything about)—our personalities seem to be something that God gave us so that we would have something to put on the altar and offer to Him." (157)

"Obedience is not wasted on Him or lost on Him." (161)

Questions for Discussion and Application:
1. How does excessive focus on our personality type tempt us not to deal with our sins properly? Is it okay to take personality tests?

2. Do you think people actually fit into nice, neat little personality types, such as Meyers-Briggs or the Enneagram? Why do you think people naturally enjoy these kinds of constructs? What's the problem with these kinds of tests? What's the problem with their authors?

3. Compare and contrast how the Bible talks about strengths and weaknesses with how a test might. What are the kinds of tasks you feel you are going above and beyond the call of duty to do because of your personality?

4. Since all things are from God, how should that change how we think about ourselves and our personalities? Should we ignore personalities entirely or should we simply think of them in a different way?

Study the Word:
Read Phil. 3:7-14 and Gal. 2:19-20. How has Paul's identity changed? What were the kinds of things he was defined by before? How is he defined now?

MISUNDERSTOOD PRINCESS

Summary:
Being a child of the King is not about feeling special or having a rhinestone-pillowed life, but is instead about serving the Kingdom, and, like Jesus, the King's son, growing through trials and suffering.

Highlights:

"While it is a great honor, being a daughter of the King is more like wearing a shirt that says STAFF boldly across the back." (165)

"How many ministries in this world have been started by people who went through something awful themselves and found both a gaping need and their own ability to do something about it? How many Christians have turned pain in their life into comfort for others?" (168)

Questions for Discussion and Application:

1. Have you heard the princess metaphor or something similar in your Christian circles?

2. Does secular culture have its own version of the princess syndrome? What are some similar metaphors? Why do you think people nowadays want to buy this idea?

3. How does God treat his children according to the author of Hebrews (Heb. 12)?

4. What are some of the painful things that you have seen that make people eager to minister to others? What are the kinds of ways you have

been better prepared for life because of a trial? What are some trials that left you or other people around you bitter and less fruitful?

Study the Word:
Read 1 Cor. 4:8; 2. Thess. 1:5; Jas. 2:5; Rev. 1:6, 5:10. Why does the New Testament use the language of royalty to talk about our identity in Christ? What does it mean to be a king? What does it mean to be a priest? What are some things we do in our mundane lives that are priestly and kingly work?

19

YOUR FAMILY TREE

Summary:

We are not isolated individuals but members of a Christian family, from whom we can learn much godliness and virtue.

Highlights:

"I am not reading their virtues as mine, I am accepting their Christ as my Christ. The Spirit who was in them is in me. His holiness was their holiness, His strength their strength. I am accepting that what He has done in others He can do in me." (174)

"Your Christian brothers and sisters have stories, and all those stories have one Giver. Love Him, love them, and be shaped." (177-8)

Questions for Discussion and Application:
1. How does the current American church discount Christians from previous generations? How does it think about history and the saints that have gone before us?

2. When we worship, whom do we worship with (Heb. 12:22-23, Rev. 4-5)?

3. How does remembering the saints that have gone before us change how we see the world and history? What kind of view of history have you had before now?

4. What are some of your favorite books about missionaries or great men of the faith? Why do you admire them?

Study the Word:

Read 1 Cor. 4:14-17. We are very familiar with how important fathers are for children. How are they important for the wider community according to Paul? Why are these examples so important?

20

LIKE SO MANY MONKEYS

Summary:
Our emotions are not guides that should lead us, but are more like monkeys that we need to coral and keep inside their cages, so that we control them, and they do not control us.

Highlights:
"Your innermost thoughts and treasured emotions are probably deceitful little monkeys that are doing (faithfully, effectively, and diligently) the work of the enemy in your life." (183)

"We choose the monkeys and all their shenanigans over Christ and His perfect leadership. We believe that the monkeys, however ugly they may be, are being honest." (184)

"Ask [God] to give you nerves of steel as you walk past the cages of the howling, disobedient, and ugly monkeys and follow Him." (185)

Questions for Discussion and Application:
1. How has everyone downstream of Sartre taught us to think of feelings as authoritative? Are feelings facts? Are feelings trustworthy? Can feelings be controlled? Can feelings be trained?

2. Can you think of any stories or movies (or real life) in which characters are encouraged to use their intuition or feelings to figure something out? Why do you think people like to "go with their gut," rather than with their head?

3. How do the Psalms train our emotions properly? How do they handle feelings of sadness and desperation, as well as feelings of joy and thankfulness? Over a third of the Psalms are considered "psalms of lament": with what

emotion do such psalms conclude? Cf. Psalms 4, 17, 70, 139 (and many more).

4. What's the proper relationship between emotion and truth (between tears and reason)?

5. What are some feelings that you wish you didn't have more often? What are concrete ways you can fight those feelings? What habits can you establish that help you resist those feelings?

Study the Word:
Read Jas. 1:2-8. How does James describe doubting? Are our prayers full of confidence that God will answer in the right way?

21

BODY IMAGE

Summary:
Your body is not something you need either to ignore or transform because it "isn't ideal." Instead it is a gift to be grateful for, and it's to be used for God's glory.

Highlights:
"The same eyes that we use to look longingly at others and resent the profound gifts that we have been given are themselves enormous gifts." (189)

"Christians glorify God when they are able to look in the mirror at their bodies—with all their faults and flaws and foibles—and truly love the One who gave it to them. That is the measure of a healthy body image." (191)

"Stop trying to image the imaginary woman you think you could be in the mirror and start trying to faithfully image your God." (193)

Questions for Discussion and Application:
1. Why are women especially vulnerable to being anxious about their body? How much influence does advertising have in how women think about the idealized body?

2. Have you ever been insecure about your body? Should you allow random marketing directors to influence how you feel about your body?

3. We are not gnostics who believe that matter is evil and anything non-material is good. What does God think about your body? What are bodies for? (Cf. 1 Cor. 6:19-20, 10:31; 2 Cor. 5:1-8; 1 Tim. 4:8)

4. Have you ever known someone in the grasp of anorexia or obesity? Or controlled by body-image perfectionism? How does the truth of the Gospel apply to them?

Study the Word:

Read Genesis 1:26-31. What does God say about the physical humans He has created? What were Adam and Eve to do with their bodies? How does that apply to us today?

22

TURN TO CHRIST

Summary:
Even though our life may be a mess and our circumstances may be messed up, we still need to turn to Christ, because we are made, not to focus on ourselves, but to focus on Him so that we might be transformed and become more like Him.

Highlights:
"Would you like to be transformed into His image with an ever-increasing glory? Would you

like to be free? Because here we are being called to freedom and to glory—and what does it take for us to get there? It takes us turning to Christ as we contemplate the Lord's glory. We look to Christ. We live to Christ. We live to Him, and consequently we can live in a state of ever-increasing glory." (199)

Questions for Discussion and Application:
1. Does God give us the answer to all our problems? How does God give us all that we need without tidily resolving every challenge we face in our lifetime?

2. How do we look to Christ in a time of trial? How can we use Scripture to gaze at Christ? How can we use prayer to gaze at Christ?

3. Have you ever been in a place where you felt lonely or without purpose? Have you ever been sick or injured for a long time? How did Christ sustain you during that time? What helped you to look and live to Christ in that time?

Study the Word:
Read 2 Cor. 3:4-18. What two things is Paul comparing in this passage? What Bible character

does Paul compare believers to? What is glory like according to this passage?

STUCK

Summary:

We often like to pursue the way of the self just because we stubbornly like to do so, even if we're stuck doing that. However, at any moment we can turn from the self to God.

Highlights:

"When you rummage into a sin corner ... you feel like you are still being brave and independent. Even after it ceases to feel free or fun anymore, at least you are being 'yourself.'" (203-204)

"If you turn away from God, you have turned away from your best self." (206)

"Turn back to God. Glorify Him. Not as some kind of a helper for you, or as an emotional support. Glorify Him as God, as the One who spoke you from nothing." (206-207)

Questions for Discussion and Application:
1. Why do human beings not like to admit they have made a mistake?

2. How, ironically, does the pursuit of self-actualization not result in your best self? Have you seen this happen? Have you seen the opposite happen to Christians who turn to God?

3. Do you tend to get stuck in any particular obstinate "sin corners"?

4. What is the process of repentance as described in John 3:16-21?

Study the Word:
Read Rom. 5:1-5. Once we have been justified by faith, what do we have? What two things, in that context, can we do?

24

BEIGE AND BORING

Summary:
We think that becoming more like Christ means becoming more bland and pietistic, overworked with pursed lips and frowns. The opposite is in fact the true: we become more interesting the more we pursue Christ.

Highlights:
"Far from getting flattened into a beige brick mold, we are being glorified through all manner

of means into something consistent with our older brother. We are being conformed, but it is being conformed into an everlasting glory." (213) "Your ultimate options are to be in your self-made costume in Hell, or in your real self, re-made in Christ and in Heaven." (213)

Questions for Discussion and Application:

1. Why do we tend to think that become more Christ-centered will make us "boring"? Does this have to do with how unbelieving culture describes godliness? What sin does the desire to avoid being "boring" or "uncool" or "unimportant" play off of?

2. Jesus and Paul did not "self-actualize." How do the Scriptures talk about maturity, e.g., sanctification, holiness, running to win the prize, and the fruits of the Spirit?

3. Are the headstrong, self-focused people among your family and friends actually the most "interesting" and pleasant people to be around in real life?

4. In whose company do you find rest, peace, and encouragement to love and good works?

Discuss books or movies which display Christian maturity.

Study the Word:
Read Hebrews 5:5-9 and 12:3-17. What does becoming like Jesus look like? Is suffering a sign that God is angry with you? Why does God discipline his children?

25

DEATH OF SELF

Summary:

We need to die to the self, because we are sinners who constantly want to pursue our own way, but God has redeemed us and changes us so we can live for Him.

Highlights:

"We have to see us being seen by Him. There it is—our pitiful self, quivering like the ugly, little mass of worthlessness that it is—and we have to acknowledge what all of our lies and confusion

were defending. What we are so afraid to see"
(221)

"God did not save us because we were so valu-
able. We have value because He saved us." (222)

"[God] will not let us keep our death but instead
breaks open our hands and our hearts and fills
them with life everlasting. Glorious, free, clean,
holy life." (223-224)

Questions for Discussion and Application:
1. Why do you suppose Christians buy books like
Girl, Wash Your Face? When it talks about valu-
ing yourself, what does the Evangelical church
get wrong about sin and grace?

2. Why do we not like to see ourselves as sinners? What are your favorite excuses?

3. How does a stronger view of sin lead to a
stronger sense of joy and relief? Have the times
when you have seen yourself for what you are
been times where you turned to God in greater
praise?

DEATH OF SELF   97

4. Our life in Christ is "already/not yet." In what ways have we put off the old man already, and in what ways do we need to keep putting him off?

Study the Word:

Read Ephesians 2:1-10. What metaphor does Paul use to describe our condition outside Christ? What gifts does Christ give us because of His death? For what purpose or result has Jesus saved us?

26

NATIVE OF ANOTHER COUNTRY

Summary:

If we want our self to be transformed, we must read and love Scripture.

Highlights:

"The Word is alive, and it knows what to do with you even when you don't know what to do with it." (232)

"The most obedient you is the most truly you
you." (233)

"We claim our busy days and our tired nights
for the kingdom. We claim our lawn work and
our work days. We claim our meal prep and our
pregnancies for Christ. We plant Kingdom flags
in every place our hands find work and in every place our hearts find trouble. We claim all
of Christ for all of life, forever." (235)

Questions for Discussion and Application:
1. Why do many Christians have such a difficult
time regularly praying and regularly reading the
Word of God?

2. Are you too busy to read Scripture or pray?
When it comes to spiritual disciplines like those,
are you a perfectionist who quits, or are you a
lazy person who doesn't try?

3. Have you ever been bored reading Scripture?
Why did God gave us a book with so much weird
stuff that doesn't seem spiritually nourishing (2
Tim. 3:16-27)?

4. How does worship equip us for life? Do you worship at church every week? Have you ever prayed the psalms, the Lord's prayer, or the prayers of Paul?

Study the Word:
Read John 20:30-31, Rom. 15:4, 1 Cor. 10:11, 1 Peter 1:10, and 2 Peter 3:1-7. For whom were the Scriptures written? What are they for?

CPSIA information can be obtained
at www.ICGtesting.com
Printed in the USA
LVHW020056220222
711688LV00010B/452